GUINNESS WORLD RECORDS

CELEBRATING 60 YEARS

DIAMOND ANNIVERSARY SPECIAL

Contents

First edition foreword 5
Introduction 6

1950s 8
- First 4-min mile
- Most No.1 singles by a solo artist
- First aircraft to exceed 1,000 mph
- Oldest F1 world champion
- Most goals scored at a World Cup Finals
- First public hovercraft flight

1960s 20
- Deepest manned descent
- First man in space
- First actor to earn over $1 million for a movie
- Youngest solo artist at No.1 in US chart
- Land speed record (1964)
- First spacewalk
- Fastest jet-powered train
- First cash dispenser
- Longest long jump
- First men on the Moon

1970s 36
- Most World Cup wins by a player
- First email
- First successful arcade game
- First mobile phone call
- Fastest transatlantic flight
- First summer blockbuster movie
- First gymnast to score a perfect 10 at an Olympic Games
- Highest-grossing sci-fi series
- Heaviest twins
- Most successful songwriter in UK chart

1980s 56
- First solo summit of Everest
- First Space Shuttle flight
- First circumnavigation via both Poles
- Most active volcano

Best-selling album
Fastest time to perform 1 million taps
Largest monster truck
First Atlantic crossing by hot-air balloon
Oldest human
Longest-running puzzle videogame

1990s 78
First hypertext browser
Fastest 100 m (1991)
Tallest house of cards
First bionic arm
Most burpees in 1 hr
Coldest place in the Milky Way discovered
Fastest transatlantic commercial flight
Land speed record (1997)
Longest escalator ride
Longest car

2000s 94
Largest collection of gnomes and pixies
Fastest solo circumnavigation by sail
Largest tortoise ever
Fastest female marathon runner
Land speed record on Mars
Highest shallow dive
Longest non-stop flight by aircraft
Fastest mile on a pogo stick while juggling three balls
Longest female fingernails
Fastest 100 m (2009)

2010s 114
Tallest building
Tallest living person
Tallest rideable motorcycle
Tallest female dog
Most retweeted tweet

Long-standing records 126

OFFICIALLY AMAZING
GUINNESS

> “Whenever people congregate to talk, they will argue, and sometimes the joy lies in the arguing and would be lost if there were any definitive answer. But more often the argument takes place on a dispute of fact, and it can be very exasperating if there is no immediate means of settling the argument. Who was the first to swim the Channel? Where is England’s deepest well, or Scotland’s highest tree, or Ireland’s oldest church? How many died in history’s worst rail crash? Who gained the biggest majority in Parliament? What is the highest point in our county? What is the greatest weight a man has ever lifted? And so on. How much heat these innocent questions can raise! Guinness in producing this book hopes that it may assist in resolving many such disputes, and may, we hope, turn heat into light.”

Earl of Iveagh K.g., C.B., C.M.G.,
Chairman of Arthur Guinness Son & Co. Ltd.

Foreword from the 1955 edition of
The Guinness Book of Records

Introduction
by Craig Glenday

The *Guinness World Records* book was born out of an argument. In the early 1950s, while on a shooting trip in County Wexford, Ireland, Sir Hugh Beaver debated with his fellow hunters about which was the fastest game bird in Europe. Unable to find a reference book to settle the argument, Sir Hugh, Managing Director of the Guinness Brewery, commissioned a compendium of superlatives from Ross and Norris McWhirter, journalists (and twins) who owned an agency specializing in facts and figures. The twins' meticulous approach to investigating and ratifying world records lay at the heart of the first book, and is something that continues to this day.

Sir Hugh's motive may not have been quite as altruistic as first it might appear. An early pioneer of marketing, Sir Hugh offered the book for free to many of the 81,400 or so pubs in the UK and Ireland in an effort to increase the sales of his beloved stout. The little green hardback was meant to be a one-off giveaway, but proved itself an instant success and quickly outgrew its intended life in bars and pubs.

Today, 60 years on, Guinness World Records is a global phenomenon both in print and beyond. The book is the world's **best-selling annual**, having now sold over 130 million copies in more than 25 different languages. We are also proud to boast worldwide TV shows, interactive museums and live touring shows, in addition to our widespread presence in the media and on the web. We have an international team of adjudicators and record managers who process more than 1,000 record applications from around the world every week. Continuing with the rigorous standards set by the McWhirter twins, only the very best applications make it through to achieve a Guinness World Records title. And the aim

of being inspiring, inclusive, engaging and entertaining is still at our core.

The book you are holding now is a curated collection of 60 of the most remarkable achievements to have been awarded a Guinness World Records title, one for each year since our birth. Many of the records featured here are historic milestones, events and inventions that changed the world. Others are simply some of our fans' favourites – those popular records that have come to represent Guinness World Records. Selecting these milestones has been a difficult task; after all, we have over 40,000 incredible records in our database. But we feel that the 60 superlatives documented here encapsulate the diverse and off-beat story of Guinness World Records.

As Editor-in-Chief, I believe it's this very randomness that has propelled Guinness World Records into the 21st century. We're constantly evolving and adapting, acting as a mirror that reflects our ever-shifting society. The story of Guinness World Records is the story of humankind's desire to push itself to bigger and better things, and to set goals and achieve them, no matter how small or how large.

I hope you enjoy this record-a-year selection, but equally I'll understand if you don't agree with all my choices; we certainly like a good debate here at Guinness World Records! As the Earl of Iveagh wrote in his foreword to the original book (reproduced here on p.5), our remit is to turn the heat of argument into the light of knowledge, and it's no less relevant now than it was 60 years ago.

Craig Glenday
Editor-in-Chief,
Guinness World Records

19

50s

1954

First 4-min mile

Roger Bannister (UK) clocks a record time of 3 min 59.4 sec at Iffley Road in Oxford on 6 May 1954. The official race announcer is Norris McWhirter (far left) who, four months later, would be invited with his brother Ross to compile the first ever edition of *The Guinness Book of Records*. Bannister sets his record just in time to be included in the inaugural book.

1955

Most No.1 singles by a solo artist

Elvis Presley releases "I Forgot to Remember to Forget", the song that will give him his first ever No.1. It will be the first of a record 18 No.1s in the USA and 20 in the UK. Turning out hit after hit, it doesn't take long for Elvis to become a global phenomenon, and by 1956 he's already dubbed the "King of Rock 'n' Roll".

The star – who grew up in Memphis, Tennessee – goes on to secure many other (as yet) unbeaten world records including the **most RIAA certificates** (262), the **most platinum RIAA certificates** (82), the **most Hot 100 entries by a solo artist** (108), the **most weeks at No.1 in the US singles chart** (80 weeks), and the **most No.1 albums by a male in the US albums chart** (9).

Even after his death, Elvis continues to break records: in 1997, on the 20th anniversary of his passing, *Elvis – The Concert* becomes the **first live tour starring a deceased performer**, bringing The King back to life on stage in virtual form.

1956

First aircraft to exceed 1,000 mph

After a number of successful attempts that the cameras on the ground infuriatingly fail to capture, the British-built *Fairey Delta 2* (*FD2*) is filmed travelling at a blistering 1,811 km/h (1,132 mph) on its eighth try. Piloted by Peter Twiss (UK), this supersonic flight also claims the world air speed record, which the *FD2* will hold for more than a year.

The aircraft's innovative delta-wing design will later be incorporated into the supersonic commercial plane *Concorde*, which will claim a speed record of its own (see p.89).

1957

Oldest F1 world champion

On 4 August, El Chueco, aka Juan Manuel Fangio (Argentina), wins his final World Formula 1 Championship, aged 46 years 41 days. He can boast one of the most successful careers in F1 history, winning the World Championship of Drivers five times – a record that will only be surpassed by Michael Schumacher (Germany), with seven victories between 1994 and 2004.

1958

Most goals scored at a World Cup Finals

During the third-place World Cup play-off, Just Fontaine (France) scores four goals for his home country in their 6–3 demolition of Germany, taking his total to 13 goals for the competition. No other player has ever scored more during the World Cup Finals.

NRDC
HOVERCRAFT

1959

First public hovercraft flight

The maiden voyage by a full-sized hovercraft takes place off Cowes, Isle of Wight, UK, on 11 June. Designed by British engineer Sir Christopher Cockerell, the craft reaches a speed of 68 knots (126 km/h; 78 mph).

It's quite incredible to think that the conceptual design of this groundbreaking new vessel – assembled on the muddy floor of the inventor's boatyard – comprises an empty can of cat food, a coffee tin, a pair of kitchen scales and a vacuum cleaner set to "blow".

Although the idea of hovercraft has been around for some time by this point, Cockerell is the first to devise an effective way of trapping the crucial cushion of air needed to glide, making it a viable mode of transport.

19

60s

1960

Deepest manned descent

Jacques Piccard (Switzerland; centre) and Donald Walsh (USA; bottom) pilot the Swiss-built US Navy bathyscaphe *Trieste* – a form of submersible with a pressurized viewing sphere – to a depth of 10,911 m (35,797 ft) on 23 January. They journey into the Challenger Deep, a depression located in the Mariana Trench and the **deepest point on Earth**, which lies some 400 km (250 mi) south-west of the island of Guam in the Pacific Ocean.

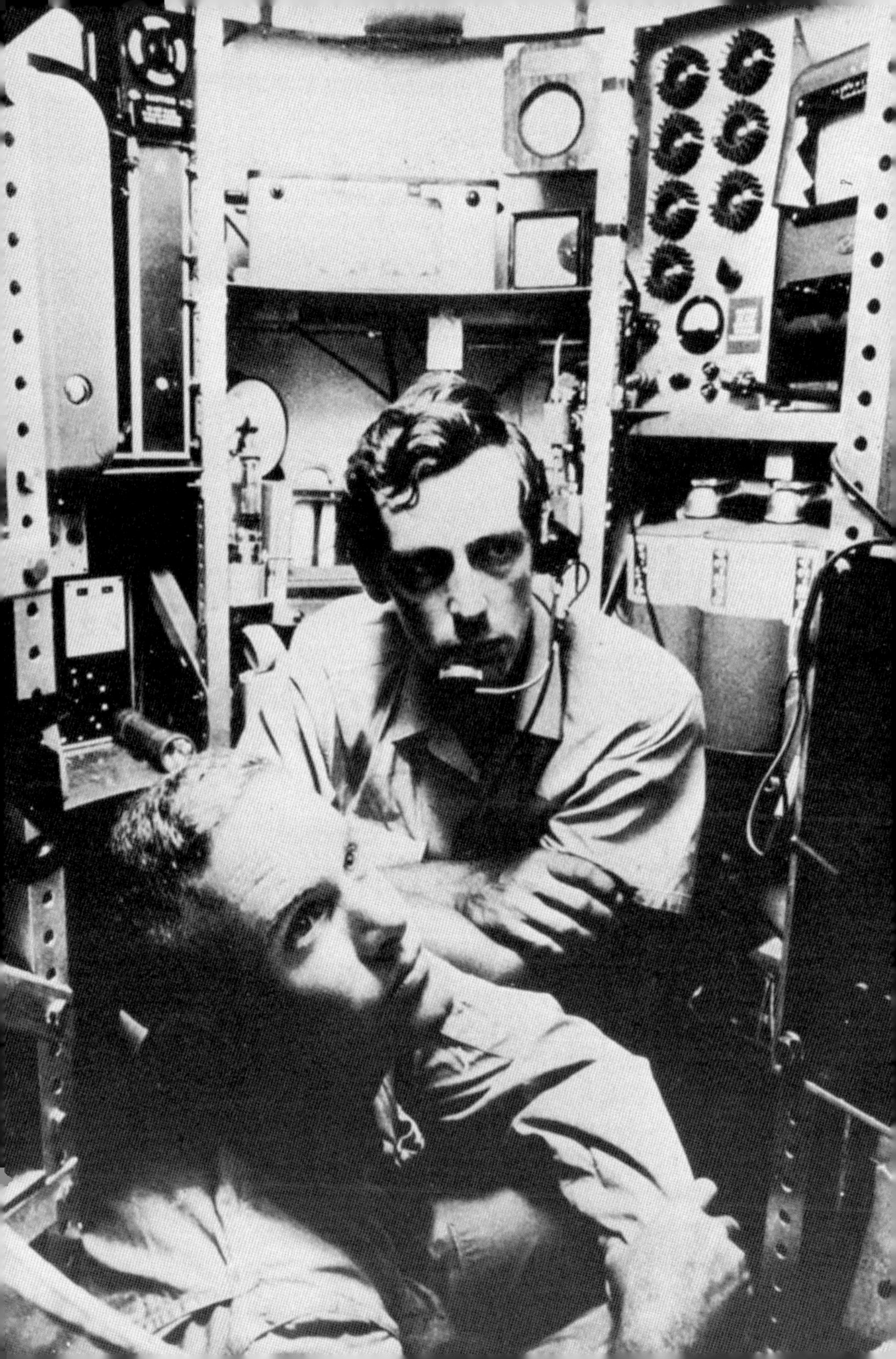

CCC

1961

First man in space

Soviet cosmonaut Yuri Gagarin becomes the **first man in space** on 12 April. He takes off in *Vostok 1* from the Baikonur Cosmodrome in Kazakhstan at 6:07 GMT and lands near Smelovka, Russia, 115 min later, having ejected by parachute. During the mission, Gagarin completes one orbit of Earth, reaching speeds of 27,400 km/h (17,500 mph).

Two schoolgirls get the shock of their lives when they see the capsule plummeting to the ground, describing it as "a huge ball, about two or three metres high. It fell, then it bounced and then it fell again. There was a huge hole where it hit the first time."

Fellow Soviet Valentina Tereshkova becomes the **first woman in space** two years later, during the *Vostok 6* orbital flight.

First actor to earn over $1 million for a movie

Celebrated actor Marlon Brando (USA) earns $1.25 million (£400,500) for his starring role as Fletcher Christian in the film *Mutiny on the Bounty*. He later goes on to break the $3-million threshold for his role in *Superman*. Another of Brando's classic films, *The Godfather*, will get its spell in the *Guinness World Records* spotlight in 2005, when the actor's copy of the script sells for $312,800 (£175,418) at Christie's auction house in London, UK, making it the **most expensive movie script** of all time.

1962

1963

Youngest solo artist at No.1 in US chart

Child prodigy Stevie Wonder (USA) is just 13 years 3 months old when his album *Recorded Live: The 12 Year Old Genius* reaches the top slot on the US album chart. Incredibly, he had been signed up to the Motown Records company at just 11 years old. Over his career, he picks up a staggering 22 Grammy Awards – more than any other solo pop performer – and in 1996 he is presented with a Grammy Lifetime Achievement Award aged just 46.

1964

Land speed record

Following in the footsteps of his father Malcolm, who was a serial record-breaker himself, Donald Campbell (UK) sets a new land speed record in jet-propelled car *Bluebird* on 17 July. Despite the damp track at Lake Eyre in South Australia, he achieves an average speed of 648.73 km/h (403.10 mph).

Not content with just conquering land, Campbell also smashes his existing water speed record on 31 December 1964 in hydroplane *Bluebird K7*, reaching an average 444.71 km/h (276.33 mph) on Lake Dumbleyung in Perth, Western Australia. To this day, he remains the only person ever to have broken both the water and land speed records in the same year.

The land speed record is now held by *Thrust SSC*, which sped to glory in 1997 (pp.90–91).

1965

First spacewalk

Having already claimed records for putting the **first satellite in space** (*Sputnik 1*, 1957) and the **first man in space** (Yuri Gagarin, 1961; see pp.24–25), the Soviet Union makes another breakthrough in 1965. Cosmonaut Lieutenant-Colonel Alexei Leonov (USSR) performs the first ever extravehicular activity (EVA) – aka spacewalk – on 18 March, spending a total of 12 min 9 sec outside the *Voskhod 2* spacecraft.

While overall the spacewalk is a success, the mission isn't seamless. When Leonov tries to return to the airlock, he finds that his spacesuit has ballooned so much during the EVA that he can't bend his arms or legs properly. To combat this, he releases a little oxygen while still in space in order to re-enter the craft. The spacewalk is an exhausting ordeal, with Leonov suffering heatstroke as a result of the exertion, although this isn't reported until later.

The first spacewalk by a US astronaut takes place the same year on 3 June. Lieutenant-Colonel Edward White conducts the EVA during the Gemini 4 mission and also encounters a problem, struggling to close the hatch on his return. White is awarded the NASA Distinguished Service Medal for this feat.

Fastest jet-powered train

Powered by two J47-19 engines, the M-497 *Black Beetle* reaches a speed of 296 km/h (183 mph) between Butler, Indiana, and Stryker, Ohio, in the USA. Built as an experimental prototype at Collinwood Yard in Cleveland, Ohio, the *Black Beetle* combines a pre-existing Budd Rail Diesel Car (RDC-3), owned by the New York Central Railroad, with boosters originally designed for the Convair B-36 Peacemaker bomber aircraft. Each booster generates approximately 7,050 Newton-metres (5,200 pound-feet) of thrust.

The same engine had been used to power Craig Breedlove's (USA) *Spirit of America* jet car to break the land speed record in 1963, before Donald Campbell rolled up in *Bluebird* the next year (pp.28–29). Nevertheless, Breedlove's car was able to claim the record for **first to exceed 400 mph over both legs of a two-leg run**.

1966

1967

First cash dispenser

The first ATM is installed at Barclays Bank in Enfield, Middlesex, UK, on 27 June. Customers are issued with paper vouchers that are fed into the machine in return for £10 notes. The first customer is actor Reg Varney, who is best known for his role in sitcom *On the Buses*.

1968

Longest long jump

Long-jumper Robert "Bob" Beamon (USA) launches himself 8.90 m (29 ft 2.5 in) at the Mexico City Olympic Games, becoming the first and only man to set the long jump record at an Olympiad, smashing the existing record by 55 cm (21.65 in).

It is the *pièce de résistance* of a fantastic season for Beamon, who had won 22 out of 23 competitions. He retains his record until 1991, when fellow US long-jumper Mike Powell leaps 8.95 m (29 ft 4.36 in) at the World Championships in Athletics held in Tokyo, Japan.

1969

First men on the Moon

At 02:56 and 15 sec GMT on 21 July, NASA astronauts Neil Armstrong and Edwin "Buzz" Aldrin, Jr (both USA) become the first people to ever set foot on the Moon. They spend two-and-a-half hours on the surface, while their colleague, Michael Collins (USA), orbits in the Command Module. They are the first of only 12 people to walk on the lunar surface to date; the **last person on the Moon** is Eugene Cernan (USA) in 1972.

19

70s

GUINNESS BOOK of RECORDS
Guinness book of r
GUINNESS BOOK OF RECORDS

1970

Most World Cup wins by a player

Having already been part of the winning team in 1958 and 1962, soccer legend Pelé (Brazil) becomes the only footballer in history to lift the trophy of the FIFA World Cup three times. He's also the **youngest player to score in the World Cup Finals**, aged 17 years 239 days when he knocks in a goal against Wales on 19 June 1958. Nine days later he becomes the **youngest player in a World Cup Final**.

1971

First email

Initiating a new era of communication, Ray Tomlinson (USA) sends the first ever email. Asked later what the message said, he says: "The test messages were entirely forgettable and I have, therefore, forgotten them."

Tomlinson plays a key part in the development of ARPANET (Advanced Research Projects Agency Network), a forerunner of the internet.

The email is seen as a speedy way for ARPANET programmers and researchers to keep in touch – particularly targeted at those who can't be relied on to answer their phones!

Speaking of the now-ubiquitous "@" symbol he adopted, Tomlinson said: "I used the '@' sign to indicate the user was 'at' some other host rather than being local."

1972

First successful arcade game

Atari founders Nolan Bushnell (pictured) and Ted Dabney (both USA) produce *Pong*, the title that gives rise to the arcade gaming craze. Based roughly on table tennis, featuring two "paddles", a white dot for a ball and a dashed line "net", it proves oddly addictive and goes on to sell more than 35,000 cabinets. The **first coin-operated *Pong* machine** is fitted at

Andy Capp's Tavern in Sunnyvale, California, and before long the locals are turning their backs on the traditional jukeboxes and pinball tables. From the start, the makers know that they have a winner on their hands.

Three years on, the trail-blazing game makes another big step, launching as a miniaturized domestic version called *Home Pong*, which is pre-installed into a console with paddle-knob controllers and can be played on TVs.

1973

First mobile phone call

On 3 April, Martin Cooper (USA), head of research at Motorola, makes the landmark call to rival, Joel Engel (USA), his counterpart at Bell Labs. He uses the phone while walking around New York City, receiving more than a few strange looks from passers-by!

This prototype cellphone will eventually become the **first commercially available mobile** – the DynaTAC 8000X – when it goes on sale in 1983. The 8000X weighs in at a hefty 785 g (28 oz) and measures 300 x 44 x 89 mm (13 x 1.75 x 3.5 in), hence why its creators affectionately nickname it "The Brick".

1974

Fastest transatlantic flight

On 1 September, USAF Major James V Sullivan and Major Noel F Widdifield pilot a Lockheed SR-71A *Blackbird* into the record books with the quickest flight across the Atlantic. Their average speed on the 1-hr 54-min 56.4-sec journey between New York and London is Mach 3.2

(around 2,908.02 km/h; 1,806.96 mph). A new *Blackbird*, the SR-72, is now being developed, with plans to make it capable of Mach 6 (about 5,800 km/h; 3,600 mph). At this speed it could make London to New York in under an hour!

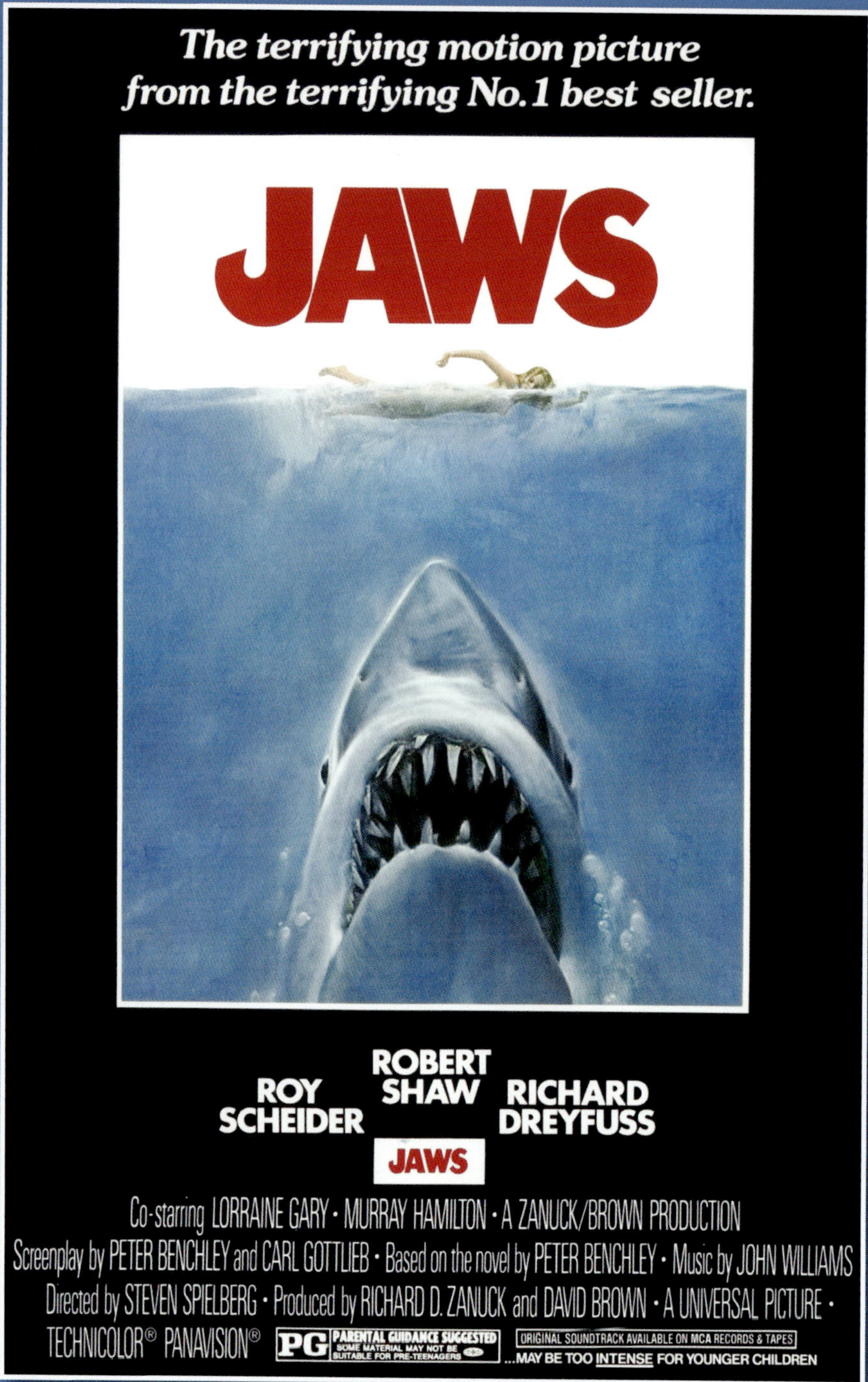

The terrifying motion picture
from the terrifying No. 1 best seller.
JAWS
ROBERT SHAW
ROY SCHEIDER
RICHARD DREYFUSS
JAWS
Co-starring LORRAINE GARY · MURRAY HAMILTON · A ZANUCK/BROWN PRODUCTION
Screenplay by PETER BENCHLEY and CARL GOTTLIEB · Based on the novel by PETER BENCHLEY · Music by JOHN WILLIAMS
Directed by STEVEN SPIELBERG · Produced by RICHARD D. ZANUCK and DAVID BROWN · A UNIVERSAL PICTURE ·
TECHNICOLOR® PANAVISION®
PG PARENTAL GUIDANCE SUGGESTED
SOME MATERIAL MAY NOT BE SUITABLE FOR PRE-TEENAGERS
ORIGINAL SOUNDTRACK AVAILABLE ON MCA RECORDS & TAPES
...MAY BE TOO INTENSE FOR YOUNGER CHILDREN

1975

First summer blockbuster movie

On 20 June, the classic horror film *Jaws* opens across multiple screens in the USA and Canada and that summer becomes one of the first films to earn $200 million at the box office. Directed by Steven Spielberg, *Jaws* is for a time the **highest-grossing movie ever** until it is surpassed by *Star Wars* in 1978 (see pp.50–51 for more on the sci-fi hit).

Spielberg goes on to direct many more blockbusters, including *Close Encounters of the Third Kind* (1977), *Jurassic Park* (1993) and *Saving Private Ryan* (1998), all of which contribute to his own record for **highest-earning film director**. According to Forbes, between 2012 and 2013 Spielberg personally nets an estimated fortune of $100 million (£62 million).

1976

First gymnast to score a perfect 10 at an Olympic Games

Nadia Comaneci (Romania) receives a perfect score for her uneven bars routine in the team competition event at the Olympic Games held in Montréal, Canada, on 18 July.

Only two other women go on to successfully match Comaneci's perfect 10: Mary Lou Retton (USA) in 1984 and Daniela Silivaş (Romania) in 1988. Owing to the International Gymnastics Federation changing the scoring system in 2006, varying scores across events and difficulty levels, Nadia's perfect score can no longer be matched.

1977

Highest-grossing sci-fi series

Packed with out-of-this-world creatures and explosive intergalactic battles, *Star Wars* makes its first appearance on the big screen on 25 May. The movie (later retitled *Star Wars: Episode IV – A New Hope*), combined with its blockbusting sequels and prequels, will pull in more than $4.55 billion (£2.75 billion) in ticket sales around the globe.

Equally impressive is the revenue generated when it returns to the big screen in 1997. *A New Hope* grosses $35,906,661 (£21,903,063) in US cinemas on the weekend of 31 January to 2 February, making it the **most profitable opening weekend for a re-released film** ever.

The success of the *Star Wars* franchise shows no signs of abating either, with the long-awaited *Episode VII* due for release in December 2015. It also breaks plenty of records outside the movie industry, with its numerous lucrative merchandise successes.

1978

Heaviest twins

Following a November weigh-in, wrestlers Billy and Benny McCrary, aka the McGuire twins, from Hendersonville, North Carolina (USA) are recognized as the world's heaviest twins. Tipping the scales at 337 kg (53 st 1 lb) and 328 kg (51 st 9 lb) respectively, they each have waists measuring 2.13 m (84 in).

Both keen bikers, the twins are shown here on a 4,830-km (3,000-mi) trip between New York

and Los Angeles. During the mini-bike road trip, the brothers meet wrestling coach Gory Guerrero, who will later train them.

They become an international phenomenon in the wrestling world, proving the decisive victors of countless bouts, with their trademark "Tupelo Splash" manoeuvre, involving one twin jumping in the air and landing on his rival with his belly!

Sadly, Billy dies aged just 32 from injuries sustained during a mini-bike stunt in 1979. Benny will live to 54, passing away in 2001.

1979

Most successful songwriter in UK chart

With 129 of the songs he has written/co-written charting in the UK, Paul McCartney (UK) lays claim to the **most songs to feature in the UK singles chart**. An astonishing 91 of his singles reach the Top 10, with 33 of those making it to No.1. Here, he is pictured with his wife, Linda, at a dinner in his honour hosted by Guinness World Records at Les Ambassadeurs Club in London on 24 October.

McCartney also boasts a number of other records, including the **first live concert broadcast to space** in 2005, the **first Bond theme nominated for a Best Original Song Oscar** ("Live and Let Die" with his band Wings in 1973) and the **most questions asked online** (he received over 3 million queries from fans during a 30-min web chat in 1997).

And that's before even taking into account the 20-plus shared records that he earned with a little help from his friends, The Beatles...

GUINNESS
BOOK OF
RECORDS
Paul McCartney M.B.

19

1980 EDITION
1983 EDITION
THE GUINNESS BOOK OF RECORDS 1988
THE GUINNESS BOOK OF RECORDS
GUINNESS BOOK OF RECORDS
1980 EDITION
GUINNESS
THE GUINNESS BOOK OF RECORDS 1987
THE GUINNESS BOOK OF RECORDS 1988
THIS WORLD
GUINNESS BOOK OF RECORDS
THE GUINNESS BOOK OF RECORDS 1985
THE GUINNESS BOOK OF RECORDS 1987
OUT OF THIS WORLD
GUINNESS
THE GUINNESS BOOK OF RECORDS

80s

OUT OF THIS WORLD
GUINNESS BOOK OF RECORDS
GUINNESS BOOK OF RECORDS
1983 EDITION
GUINNESS BOOK OF RECORDS
THE GUINNESS BOOK OF RECORDS 1985
GUINNESS BOOK OF RECORDS
THE GUINNESS BOOK OF RECORDS 1988
THE GUINNESS BOOK OF RECORDS
GUINNESS BOOK OF RECORDS
1980 EDITION
GUINNESS
THE GUINNESS BOOK OF RECORDS

1980

First solo summit of Everest

On 20 August, nearly three decades after Edmund Hillary (New Zealand) and Tenzing Norgay (India/Tibet) become the first to scale Earth's highest peak in 1953, Italian adventurer Reinhold Messner becomes the first to conquer Mount Everest alone. He later admits it was one of the hardest feats he had ever undertaken: "I was in continual agony; I have never in my whole life been so tired as on the summit of Everest. I just sat there, oblivious

to everything… I knew I was physically at the end of my tether." Having already completed the challenge two years previously with Peter Habeler, his solo ascent takes three days from base camp at 6,500 m (21,325 ft). What's more extraordinary is that both his Everest climbs are made without the aid of bottled oxygen.

Having grown up in the Italian Dolomites, accompanying his father on many a challenging climb as a teenager, he learns to survive at high altitudes from a young age. Messner goes on to tackle many more of the planet's most challenging peaks, as well as extreme terrains such as Antarctica and the Gobi Desert.

1981

First Space Shuttle flight

NASA's *Columbia* makes its maiden orbital flight between 12 and 14 April. The mission, officially designated STS-1, marks the start of a run of 27 successful flights for *Columbia*.

In total, there will be five Space Shuttles built (*Columbia* is proceeded by *Challenger*, *Discovery*, *Atlantis* and *Endeavour*), which together will complete 135 missions, until their retirement in 2011. The combined mission time for these workhorse, off-planet transporters is 1,322 days 19 hr 21 min 23 sec.

As the **first reusable spacecraft**, the Space Shuttles carry out every conceivable role over their career, including satellite launches and recovery, astronaut transit and supply carrier. They are also instrumental in the ten-year project to build the **largest artificial satellite**, the *International Space Station*.

Tragically, on 1 February 2003, during its 28th mission, *Columbia* disintegrates while re-entering the Earth's atmosphere, killing all seven crew members.

1982

First circumnavigation via both Poles

Sir Ranulph Fiennes and Charles Burton (both UK) complete the **first surface circumnavigation via both geographical Poles** on 29 August. Their British Trans-Globe Expedition travels south from Greenwich, London, UK, on 2 September 1979, crosses the South Pole on 15 December 1980, and the North Pole on 10 April 1982, before returning to Greenwich to complete their incredible 56,000-km (35,000-mi) journey.

1983

Most active volcano

On 3 January, lava begins to explode from a fissure in the Kilauea shield volcano on Big Island, the southernmost island of Hawaii, USA. Kilauea spews lava at an astonishing rate of up to 5 m^3 (176 cu ft) per second and continues erupting to the present day.

Kilauea is the youngest of the many volcanoes that make up the archipelago. Indeed, the island chain owes its very existence to the high rate of geothermal activity in the region, positioned as it is above a "hot spot" in the Earth's crust. Hawaii boasts a number of other volcanic records, including the **largest active volcano** (Mauna Loa, a neighbour of Kilauea) and the **longest lava cave**, the 59.3-km-long (36.9-mi) Kazumura Cave located within Kilauea itself.

Michael Jackson
Thriller

1984

Best-selling album

Thriller by Michael Jackson (USA) picks up eight Grammy awards, including Album of the Year and Record of the Year (for the single "Beat It"), and goes on to become the **best-selling album of all time**.

The "King of Pop" will become a regular feature in the pages of *Guinness World Records*, earning multiple certificates for, among other things, the **longest span of US top 40 singles** (39 years 2 months), **largest TV audience for a music video premiere** (500 million for "Black or White") and the **most charities supported by a pop star** (39).

In 2006, Jackson pays a visit to GWR's London headquarters (see inset) to deliver a personal thank you to the team and to receive copies of all his world record certificates. He remains a good friend of GWR until his untimely death in 2009 at the age of 50.

NIKE
1
MILLION
TO GO

1985

Fastest time to perform 1 million taps

Roy Castle (UK, 1932–94), host of the BBC TV programme *Record Breakers* from 1972 to 1993, sets a record of his own, tap dancing for 23 hr 44 min at the Guinness World of Records Exhibition in Piccadilly, London, UK.

The thrill of being immersed in the world of record-breaking clearly rubs off on Roy. He later earns the titles for **most people in a chorus line** shared with 592 other dancers (since beaten) and **longest time wing walking**, spending 3 hr 23 min on a Boeing Stearman biplane flying from London to Paris in 1990 – a feat which has yet to be surpassed.

1986

Largest monster truck

Summer sees the unveiling of *Bigfoot 5* (pictured in 2006), built by Bob Chandler of St Louis, USA, who is generally considered the father of the monster-truck industry. *Bigfoot 5* makes a dwarf of any other 4x4 at a staggering 4.7 m (15 ft 6 in) tall. Its gigantic tyres alone stand some 3 m (10 ft) high and the supersized truck weighs in at 17,200 kg (38,000 lb).

Initially born out of Chandler's passion for off-road driving – and to demonstrate the potential of four-wheel-drive vehicles to customers at his 4x4 dealership – this record-breaking pickup is the fifth iteration. Each new member of the *Bigfoot* family incorporates cutting-edge technology, materials and innovative designs, in order to stay at the forefront of the monster-truck world. The fleet now stands at 20 trucks, with number 21 currently under construction, but number five remains the biggest of them all.

1987

First Atlantic crossing by hot-air balloon

On 2 July, Richard Branson (UK) and pilot Per Lindstrand (Sweden) begin their daring transatlantic flight in the purpose-built *Virgin Atlantic Flyer* at Sugarloaf in Maine, USA. They arrive in Limavady in Co. Londonderry, UK, the following day, having travelled 4,947 km (3,075 mi) in just 31 hr 41 min.

Four years later, the pair take to the skies once more in the *Virgin Otsuka Pacific Flyer*, a behemoth of a balloon with an envelope volume of 73,600 m^3 (2.6 million cu ft). They venture from Japan to Lac la Matre in Yukon, Canada, and enter the record books for **first Pacific crossing by hot-air balloon**. They complete the journey in 46 hr 15 min – at times reaching speeds in excess of 320 km/h (200 mph).

1988

Oldest human

On 11 January, France's Jeanne Calment, who was born on 21 February 1875, becomes the **oldest living person**.

At the age of 112, the supercentenarian (pictured here in 1995) attributes her longevity to a wide range of factors, from her genes and regular exercise to applying olive oil to her skin. That said, she is also a fan of chocolate and spent most of her life as a smoker.

Two years later, Calment becomes the **oldest ever actress**, when she plays herself in the 1990 film *Vincent and Me*, aged 114. She is considered the last living person to have met eminent Dutch artist Vincent Van Gogh, upon whom the movie is based.

Incredibly, she lives until 1997, reaching the grand old age of 122 years 164 days, making her the **oldest person ever**.

TETRIS™
PUSH START
© 1989 Nintendo
Hatris™

1989

Longest-running puzzle videogame

Tetris, an experimental videogame created back in 1984 on an Elektronika 60 terminal computer by Alexey Pajitnov (USSR/Russia), makes its debut on the Nintendo Game Boy, triggering an international craze of virtual brick-stacking. Over its 30-year history, the seriously addictive game goes on to sell more than 30.26 million copies – making it the **best-selling puzzle videogame of all time** – and picks up many other records, including the **first videogame played in space** and **most ported videogame**, with more than 65 versions across different platforms.

1991
RECORDS
1992
THE GUINNESS BOOK OF RECORDS 199
The New Guinness Book of Records 1995
994
THE
GUINNESS

19

90s

1994
THE GUINNESS BOOK OF RECORDS
GUINNESS RECORDS
GUINNESS BOOK OF RECORDS
WORLD BEST SELLER
GUINNESS
BOOK OF RECORDS
RECORDS

1990

First hypertext browser

While working at the CERN European Particle Physics Laboratory near Geneva, Switzerland, computer scientist Tim Berners-Lee (UK) creates the first hypertext browser, which launches a year later as the "WorldWideWeb". By October 1990, he has formulated the core components of the global network that we still use to this day: HTML, URL and HTTP.

Although the World Wide Web is initially devised as a speedy means for scientists around the globe to share their research, Berners-Lee quickly realizes that its potential goes far beyond the academic community.

Of course, the web is now an integral part of our everyday lives, used for reading/reporting the latest news, keeping in touch with friends, shopping, music and movies – and even applying for Guinness World Records!

1991

Fastest 100 m

Thirty-year-old Carl Lewis (USA) clocks a record-breaking time of 9.86 sec in the 100 m final at the Athletics World Championships in Tokyo, Japan – a record now held by Usain Bolt (see pp.112–113). Along with Bolt, Lewis also holds the title for the **most wins of the 100 m at the Olympics**, having claimed the gold medal twice.

Tallest house of cards

In Spirit Lake, Iowa, Bryan Berg (USA) builds a 75-storey house of cards that stands 4.42 m (14 ft 6 in) high. This sets a record that he will later break on a further nine occasions. His loftiest success comes in 2007, with the tower of cards soaring to 7.86 m (25 ft 9 in)!

1992

1993

First bionic arm

Scottish hotel owner Campbell Aird is fitted with a cutting-edge limb created by a team of five bio-engineers at the Margaret Rose Hospital in Edinburgh, UK. The prosthetic is a great leap forward in the field as it is powered by a complex network of state-of-the-art electric motors, gears and microchips. It offers far more realistic movement than anything that has preceded it, and is controlled by electrical impulses sent directly from Aird's brain.

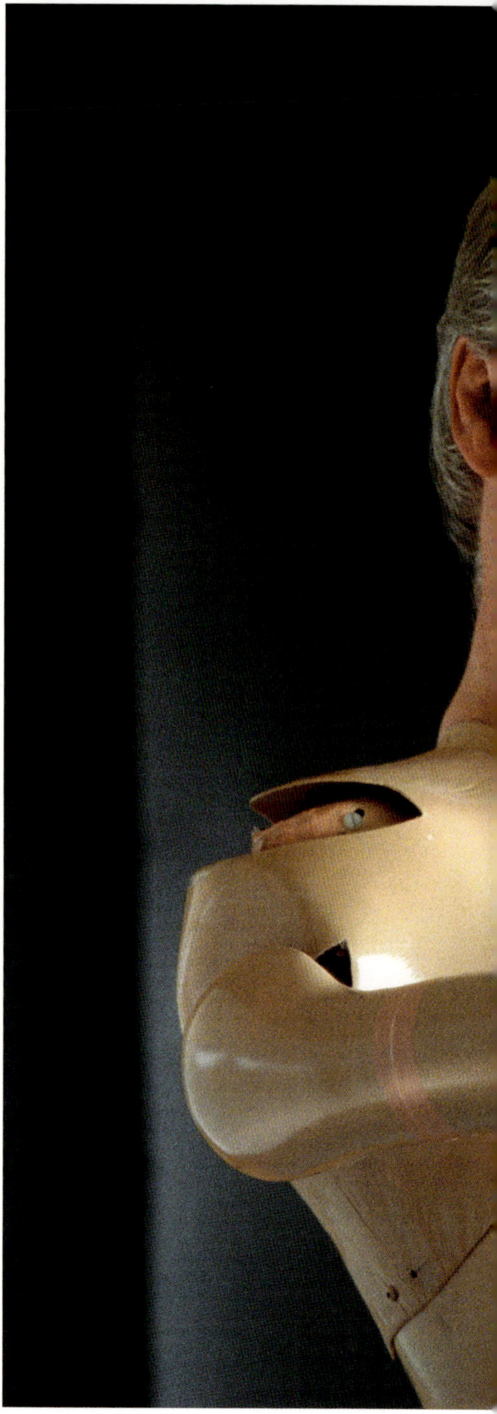

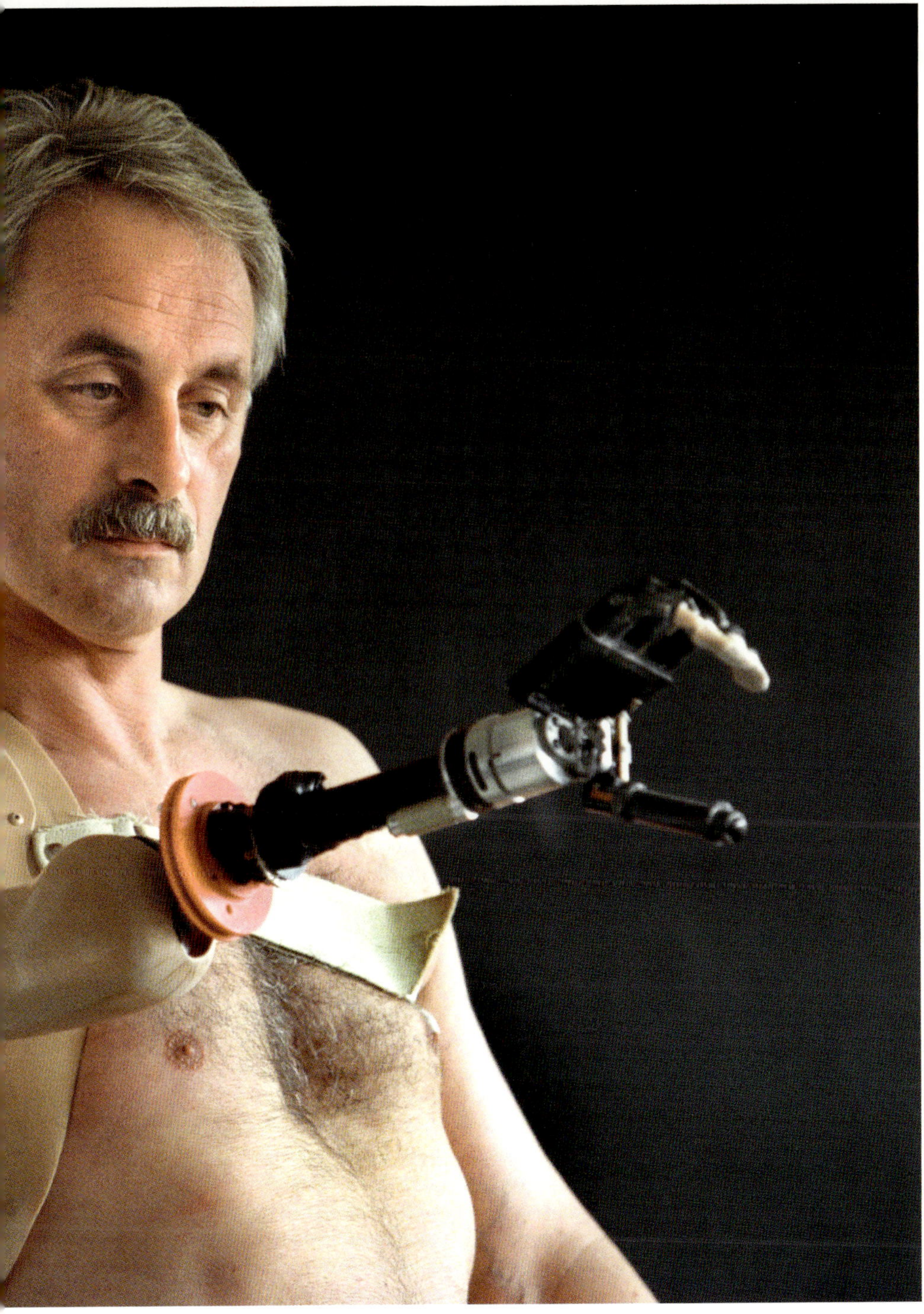

GB

1994

Most burpees in 1 hr

On 4 February, Paddy Doyle (UK) completes 1,840 para-jumps (burpees) in 60 min. The manoeuvre begins in a standing position, then drops to a squat position with hands on the ground, kicking the feet back, and then returns to a squat before ending on the feet again. It was developed by American physiologist Royal Burpee as part of a fitness test.

Super-fit Doyle is no stranger to endurance records and has dozens of titles under his belt, including **most full-contact kicks in 1 hr** (5,750), **most push-ups in 12 hr** (19,325), **most squats in 1 min carrying a 100-lb pack** (38) and **fastest marathon cross-country with a 40-lb pack** (6 hr 28 min 22 sec).

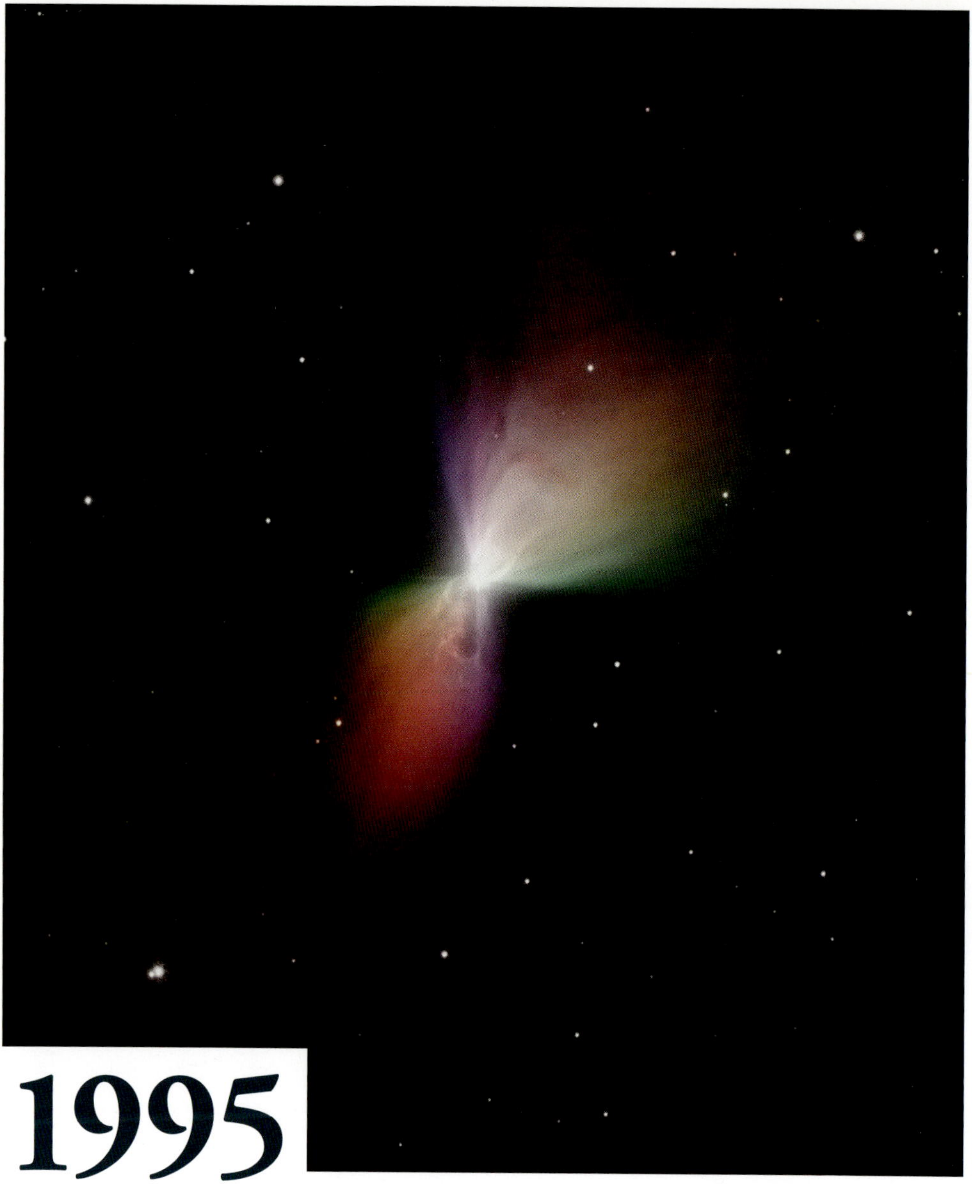

1995

Coldest place in the Milky Way discovered

Using data obtained by the Space Observatory-Submillimeter radio telescope in La Silla, Chile, astronomers identify the chilliest location in our galaxy. The Boomerang Nebula, a cloud of dust and gases that lies some 5,000 light years from Earth, has a temperature of -272°C (-457.6°F), which is only marginally warmer than absolute zero: -273.15°C (-459.67°F).

Fastest transatlantic commercial flight

On 7 February, a British Airways *Concorde* zips between New York and London in just 2 hr 52 min 59 sec, covering 6,035 km (3,750 mi). The plane, piloted by Captain Leslie Scott (UK), averages 2,010 km/h (1,250 mph).

A marvel of engineering, inspired by the design of pioneering jet planes such as the *Fairey Delta 2* (see pp.14–15), *Concorde* has a capacity of 100 passengers and will carry some 2.5 million people during its lifespan. While in supersonic flight the plane can stretch up to 25 cm (10 in), so a special paint is developed to tolerate both expansion and the intense heat.

The aircraft is retired in 2003, owing to a lack of financial support for required updates. Many attribute this reticence to invest to a slump in *Concorde*'s popularity following the crash of Air France *Concorde* Flight 4590 in 2000.

1996

1997

Land speed record

The official fastest car measured over one mile (aka the land speed record) reaches an as-yet-unbeaten 1,227.985 km/h (763.035 mph) (Mach 1.02) on 15 October, when driver Andy Green (UK) powers *Thrust SSC* to glory in the Black Rock Desert, Nevada, USA.

Along with project director Richard Noble, professional fighter pilot Green is now a core part of the team working on the *Bloodhound SSC*. It's hoped that this new supersonic car, with Green at the wheel, will be able to break the 1,000-mph (1,600-km/h) barrier at Hakskeen Pan, a dried-out lake in South Africa. Two trial runs are slated for 2015 and 2016.

1998

Longest escalator ride

Suresh Joachim (Sri Lanka/Canada) travels 225.4 km (140 mi) up and down the escalators at Westfield Shopping Centre in Burwood, New South Wales, Australia, on 25–31 May.

Proving that he can go the distance, Joachim also holds the titles for **longest time rocking a rocking chair** (75 hr 3 min) and the **longest continuous crawl** (56.62 km; 35.18 mi).

1999

Longest car

Designed by Jay Ohrberg of Burbank, California, USA, *American Dream* is the 30.5-m (100-ft), 26-wheeled juggernaut of the limousine world. Featuring a king-sized water bed, a helipad and even a swimming pool with diving board, it can be driven as a rigid vehicle (as pictured) or re-set to bend in the middle.

While the planet's longest car is obviously one of his crowning achievements, Ohrberg has built dozens of other amazing automobiles, hence his nickname "King of the Show Cars". His unique vehicles even appear in films such as *Batman Returns*, *RoboCop*, *Back to the Future* and TV series *Knight Rider* (in which he himself starred in several episodes).

As well as designing awe-inspiring cars for Hollywood for a living, Ohrberg has created over 500 experimental models, such as the *Pink Panther Limo*, *Bathtub Car* and, of course, *American Dream*, as personal projects. He hopes to some day display all of his incredible automobiles in a dedicated museum.

20
HUNDREDS OF NEW RECORDS INSIDE!
GUINNESS WORLD RECORDS 2009
GUINNESS WORLD RECORDS 2000
GUINNESS WORLD RECORDS
GUINNESS WORLD RECORDS 2006
GUINNESS WORLD RECORDS
2007

00s

2000

Largest collection of gnomes and pixies

Since the turn of the 21st century, large collections have been one of the quickest-growing categories at Guinness World Records. Here, Ann Atkin (UK) is surrounded by her army of 2,010 gnomes and pixies. The gnome devotee goes on to break her own record,

and at the last count, her collection stands at 2,042. All of her garden ornaments live in a 1.6-hectare (four-acre) beechwood "Gnome Reserve" that is visited by 25,000 people every year. If you're thinking of dropping by, be prepared to be handed a pointy hat before entering – "so as not to embarrass the gnomes that live there!". Atkin's favourite is a gnome called "Siegfried", which she sculpted herself back in 1978.

2001

Fastest solo circumnavigation by sail

On 11 February, Ellen MacArthur (UK) completes a singlehanded circumnavigation of the globe in her yacht *Kingfisher*, having sailed 38,600 km (24,000 mi) in a record 94 days 4 hr 25 min 40 sec. Not only is this her first Guinness World Records title, but she also receives an MBE for

her services to sport. MacArthur goes on to beat her own record in 2005, circumnavigating in her trimaran *B&Q* from Ushant, France, in just 71 days 14 hr 18 min 33 sec. For this, she is knighted and also receives the French *Legion d'Honneur.* Although Dame Ellen loses the absolute record in 2008 – when Francis Joyon (France) shaves a staggering 14 days off her time – she remains the **fastest female sailor to circumnavigate the world**.

2002

Largest tortoise ever

The world mourns the death of Goliath, a Galápagos giant. Resident at the Life Fellowship Bird Sanctuary in Seffner, Florida, USA, the world's largest tortoise was 135.8 cm (4 ft 5 in) long and 102 cm (3 ft 4 in) wide, and weighed in at a hefty 417 kg (920 lb).

Galápagos tortoises are also known for their longevity. One individual in captivity is recorded as living for 152 years, although some think it may have been even older.

Today, the largest subpopulation of these endangered reptiles resides on Isabela Island. The archipelago is named after these amazing creatures – "galápago" is "tortoise" in Spanish.

2003

Fastest female marathon runner

On 13 April, British athlete Paula Radcliffe sets an unprecedented time of 2 hr 15 min 25 sec at the London Marathon. On realizing the record is at stake, she sprints the final 800 m in 2 min 25 sec. She also boasts the **fastest time to run the Chicago Marathon** (2 hr 17 min 18 sec) and the **fastest 10 km road run** (30 min 21 sec), set in San Juan, Puerto Rico, also in 2003.

Land speed record on Mars

The twin NASA Mars Exploration Rovers, *Spirit* and *Opportunity*, touch down on the surface of the Red Planet on 4 and 25 January 2004 respectively. Each is capable of a maximum velocity of 5 cm/sec (1.9 in/sec), earning them the land speed record on Mars.

After successfully landing, the rovers study incredible phenomena including dust devils, hydrothermal vents and several meteorites. Communication with *Spirit* is lost in 2010, but *Opportunity* continues to speed across the planet to this day.

2004

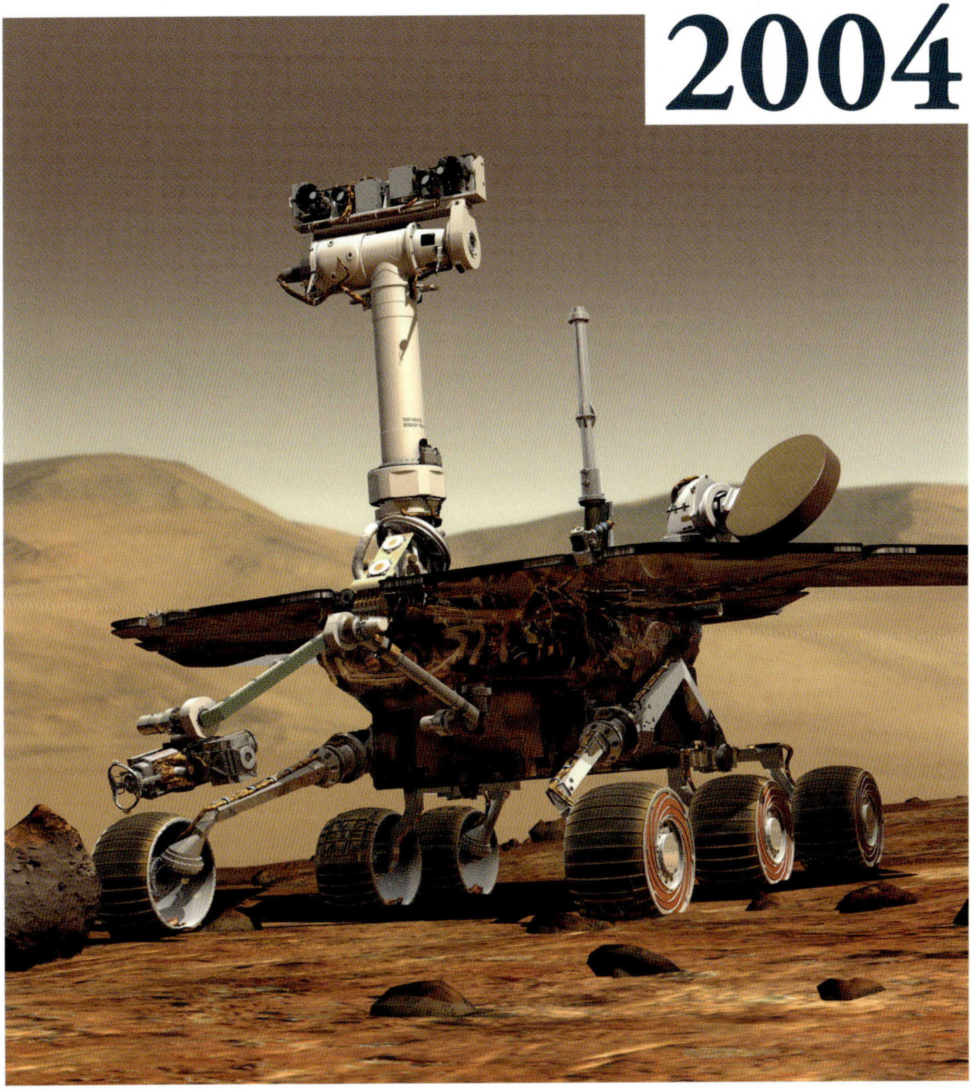

2005

Highest shallow dive

Darren Taylor (USA), aka "Professor Splash", dives 10.3 m (33 ft 10 in) into a pool of water just 30 cm (12 in) deep on 22 October. He goes on to break his record numerous times, most recently surviving a 11.56-m (37-ft 11-in) plunge in September 2014!

To prove he's the master of more than one element, Taylor also achieves the record for **highest shallow dive into fire** on 21 June 2014, jumping from a height of 8 m (26 ft 3 in) into a pool of flames.

Needless to say, Taylor has many years of experience with shallow diving, so this certainly isn't one to try at home!

2006

Longest non-stop flight by aircraft

On 8 February 2006, daredevil adventurer Steve Fossett (USA) takes off from the Kennedy Space Center, Florida, USA, in the *Virgin Atlantic GlobalFlyer* aeroplane and flies 42,469.4 km (26,389.3 mi) to the UK. He intends to reach Kent International Airport, but an electrical glitch forces him to land some 280 km (170 mi) away in Bournemouth, Dorset. He touches down after 76 hr 45 min of continuous flight, beating the previous non-stop record held by the *Breitling Orbiter 3* balloon by 165.4 km (102.8 mi).

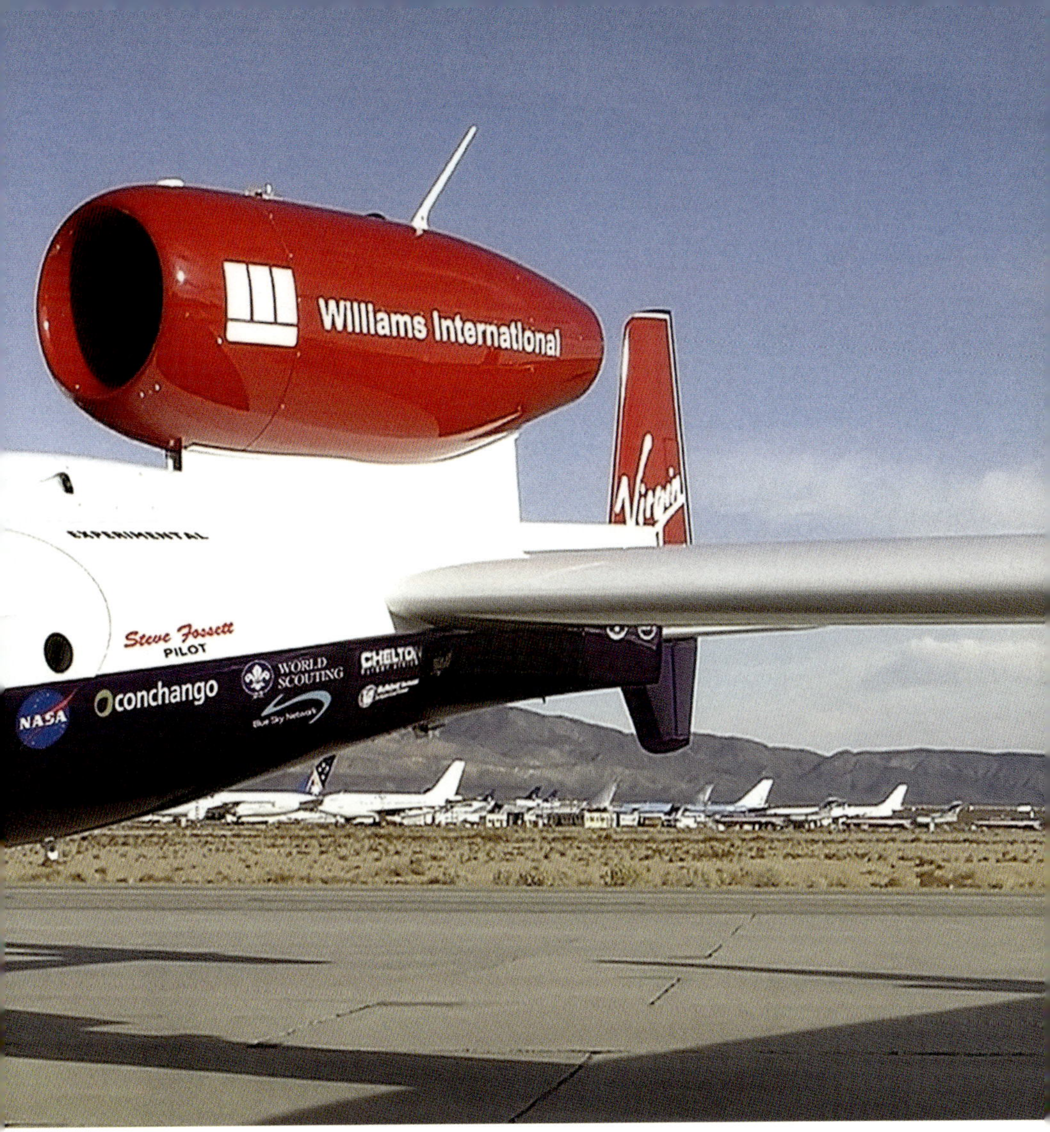

Malfunctions aside, the *GlobalFlyer* only has 90 kg (200 lb) of fuel remaining from an initial take-off load of 8,210 kg (18,100 lb).

Fossett is no stranger to the record books, achieving the **fastest solo circumnavigation by balloon** in 2002, taking just 13 days 8 hr 33 min; the **fastest speed for an airship**, at 112 km/h (69.6 mph) in 2004; and the **highest flight in a glider**, when he reaches 15,460 m (50,721 ft) above Argentina in 2006.

Tragically, in 2007, while planning his next adventure, Fossett dies in a plane crash in the Sierra Nevada mountains of California, USA – the victim of suspected down-draughts.

2007

Fastest mile on a pogo stick while juggling three balls

Ashrita Furman (USA) – who holds the Guinness World Records title for holding the **most Guinness World Records titles held** – adds another to his tally on 26 September, when he takes a mere 23 min 28 sec to hop one mile on his pogo stick along the Brooklyn Promenade

in New York while juggling, without falling or dropping a ball once (see centre of montage).

Commonly known as "Mr Versatility", owing to the mind-boggling variety of records to his name, as of 1 May 2014, Furman has set 521 records, of which 182 are still current.

Having set his first record in 1979 (completing 27,000 star jumps/jumping jacks), he hasn't looked back. As you can see from this image, his records are very diverse, ranging from **fastest mile on a space hopper** (13 min) to **farthest distance walked balancing a baseball bat on one finger** (14.48 km; 9 mi).

2008

Longest female fingernails

Lee Redmond (USA) sets a new world record on TV show *Lo Show dei Record* in Madrid, Spain, on 23 February. After nearly 30 years of growth, her nails measure a total of 8.65 m (28 ft 4.5 in); the longest nail is that on her right thumb, which alone is 90 cm (2 ft 11 in).

Sadly, Redmond loses her nails in a road accident the following year; however, she still retains the record for **longest female fingernails ever**.

TDK
Bolt
2009

2009

Fastest 100 m

On 16 August, Usain Bolt (Jamaica) shatters his own 100 m record exactly one year after taking the Olympic gold. His time of 9.58 sec shaves 0.11 sec off his previous personal best and is the fastest 100 m run ever recorded.

Bolt's top speed during the sprint is a blistering 44.72 km/h (27.79 mph). Scientists estimate his maximum power output equates to 2,619.5 watts and that 81.58 kilojoules of energy are burned by the end of the run.

Four days later, at the same IAAF World Championships, Bolt also takes the record for **fastest 200 m**, with a time of 19.19 sec.

20

EXPLODING WITH
THOUSANDS OF NEW RECORDS
BURSTING WITH
AMAZING NEW RECORDS
DISCOVER A WORLD
OF NEW RECORDS
GUINNESS
WORLD
RECORDS
2014
GUINNESS
WORLD
RECORDS
2015
OFFICIALLY AMAZING
3D

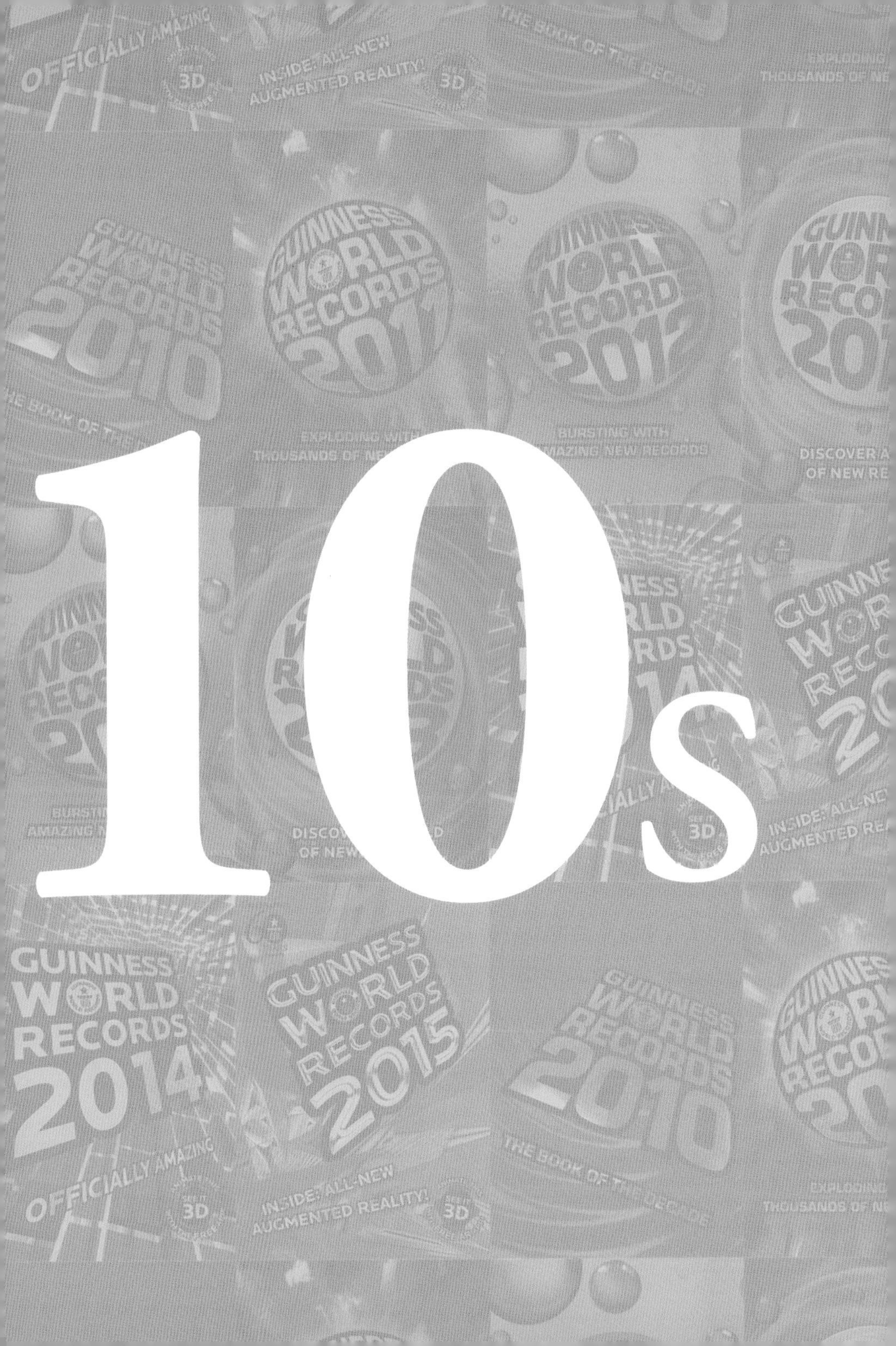
OFFICIALLY AMAZING
INSIDE: ALL-NEW AUGMENTED REALITY!
GUINNESS WORLD RECORDS 2010
THE BOOK OF THE DECADE
GUINNESS WORLD RECORDS 2014
GUINNESS WORLD RECORDS 2015
BURSTING WITH AMAZING NEW RECORDS

10s

2010

Tallest building

In 2010, the Burj Khalifa (Khalifa Tower), which measures 828 m (2,716 ft 6 in), becomes the tallest building on the planet. This is more than twice the height of the Empire State Building, and almost three times the size of the Eiffel Tower. Developed by Emaar Properties, it is officially opened in Dubai, UAE, on 4 January.

As well as laying claim to a number of other lofty records itself – such as **tallest elevator in a building** (504 m; 1,654 ft) and **highest restaurant from ground level** (441.3 m; 1,447 ft 10 in) – the mighty structure has served as the stage for many other record attempts, including **highest BASE jump from a building** and **fastest time to climb the Burj Khalifa by bicycle** (2 hr 20 min 38 sec).

However, this monumental edifice may be beaten by a Middle Eastern rival in the not-too-distant future. The Kingdom Tower, currently under construction in Jeddah, Saudi Arabia, is designed to reach 1,000 m (3,281 ft). As the world's first 1-km building, it will soar 170 m (550 ft) taller than the Burj Khalifa.

2011

Tallest living person

On 8 February, Sultan Kösen (Turkey) is measured to stand at an impressive 251 cm (8 ft 3 in) in the Turkish capital, Ankara, confirming his status as the tallest human being on Earth.

Stretching 28.5 cm (11.22 in) from the wrist to the tip of the middle finger, his hands also become record-breakers when they are verified as the **largest hands on a living person**. They span 30.48 cm (12 in) – about the size of a dinner plate!

Despite his lofty achievement, Kösen falls short of the **tallest person ever**, Robert Wadlow (USA); find out how tall he was on p.126...

OFF
DUTY
NYC TAX

2012

Tallest rideable motorcycle

Measuring 5.1 m (16 ft 8.7 in) from the ground to the top of the handlebars, this goliath motorcycle is ridden over a 100-m (328-ft) course at Montecchio Emilia, Italy, to claim the record on 24 March. Built by Fabio Reggiani (Italy), the bike is fitted with stabilizer wheels to reduce the risk of it toppling, but these are removed for the record attempt.

The motorbike's mighty dimensions don't just stop at its height. It measures 10 m (32 ft 9.6 in) long, 2.5 m (8 ft 2.4 in) wide and weighs around 5,000 kg (11,000 lb). The vehicle is on a 6:1 scale to the standard model and is powered by a 5.7-litre V8 motor, running at 280 hp.

Reggiani first conceived of the bike while visiting New Zealand in 2012. Initially he wanted to create the largest static chopper, but then decided it would be a lot more show-stopping to create one that could be ridden. He completed it in a mere six months.

2013

Tallest female dog

In October, Morgan the Great Dane (right) is crowned the world's tallest living female dog, and to mark the occasion, GWR arranges a shoot with Zeus, the **tallest male dog**. It's the first time these gentle giants have met, and they get on famously. Morgan, from Ontario,

Canada, measures 98.15 cm (3 ft 2.6 in) to the haunches (shoulders), while Zeus, from Michigan, USA, towers over her at 111.8 cm (3 ft 8 in). According to Morgan's owner, Cathy Payne, she has a mild-mannered nature, except when it comes to squirrels, which she loves to chase. Zeus is equally even-tempered, and is often mistaken for a pony! Both Morgan and Zeus sadly pass away in 2014, but Zeus still holds the record for **tallest dog ever**.

2014

Most retweeted tweet

The "selfie" might have been around for a while, but in 2014 its popularity sky-rockets. If you want proof, US TV presenter Ellen DeGeneres' snap, taken at the 2014 Academy Awards on 2 March, becomes the **most widespread social networking message** since Twitter began in 2006, with more than 1 million retweets in little over an hour. The image features a host of A-list movie stars, including Channing Tatum, Meryl Streep, Julia Roberts, Jennifer Lawrence, Bradley Cooper, Jared Leto, Kevin Spacey, Brad Pitt, Angelina Jolie, Lupita N'yongo and her brother Peter N'yongo.

Long-standing records

Much has changed in the past 60 years, but what's perhaps more amazing are those rare superlatives that have remained unchallenged. These are the records that after six decades are seemingly "unbreakable", having never been beaten since our very first edition in 1955.

Tallest man ever

The tallest man in medical history is Robert Pershing Wadlow (USA), who when last measured on 27 June 1940, was 2.72 m (8 ft 11.1 in) tall. Wadlow also had the **largest hands ever** – stretching 32.3 cm (12.75 in) from the wrist to the tip of his middle finger and requiring a size 25 ring. In addition, he had the **largest feet ever** and wore US size 37AA shoes – the equivalent of 47 cm (1 ft 6.5 in) in length.

Best-selling single

"White Christmas", by Bing Crosby (USA, 1903–77), has sold an estimated 50 million copies worldwide since its first release. The festive favourite was written by Irving Berlin in 1940, recorded in just 18 min on 29 May

1942 and was introduced in Berlin's musical movie *Holiday Inn* (USA, 1942), starring Fred Astaire and Crosby himself.

Richest person

John D Rockefeller's wealth was estimated at about $900 million (£184.88 million) in 1913, equivalent to $189.6 billion (£114.39 billion) when adjusted for inflation to today's prices.

Largest office building

The Pentagon, built to house the US government's war offices in Washington DC, remains the world's largest office building. In 1955, it was listed in our first edition as hosting 28,500 people, and by 2008 it accommodated 31,000 military, non-military and civilian employees. Each of the outermost sides is 281 m (921 ft) long and, at its widest point, the Pentagon is as wide as the Empire State Building is tall. The floor area equates to some 604,000 m^2 (6.5 million sq ft).

Highest-grossing movie

Gone with the Wind (USA, 1939) took $393.4 million (then £88 million) at the international box office. But in an inflation-adjusted list it comes top of all other movies, with total earnings of $3.44 billion (£2.10 billion). Just think how much popcorn you could buy with all that money...

Largest diamond

A fitting record to end this diamond anniversary celebration, the largest uncut diamond ever found is the "Cullinan", which weighed 3,106.75 carats when unearthed at South Africa's Premier Diamond Mine in 1905. Two of the 100-plus gems cut from the raw diamond are mounted in the British Crown Jewels, including Cullinan I – the *Great Star of Africa*.

Editor-in-Chief
Craig Glenday

Senior Managing Editor
Stephen Fall

Project Editor
Adam Millward

Senior Art Editor
Paul Oakley

Design
Jon Addison, Robert Vickers

Picture Editor
Michael Whitty

Deputy Picture Editor
Fran Morales

Talent Researcher
Jenny Langridge

VP Publishing
Jenny Heller

Director of Procurement
Patricia Magill

Publishing Manager
Jane Boatfield

Special thanks to: Neil Fitter, Mike Flynn, Amarilis Whitty

Image credits: Alamy, Corbis, Decca, Drew Gardner/GWR, Getty, John Wright/GWR, Kevin Scott Ramos/GWR, Lucasfilm, NASA/JPL/Cornell University, NOAA, PA, Paul Michael Hughes/GWR, Ranald Mackechnie/GWR, Red Bull, Reuters, Rex, Richard Bradbury/GWR, Ryan Schude/GWR, Sam Christmas/GWR, Topfoto, Universal Pictures, USA

British Library Cataloguing in Publication Data: a catalogue record for this book is available from the British Library

ISBN 978 1 908843 91 3

Printed in Germany

GUINNESS WORLD RECORDS™
OFFICIALLY AMAZING

THE JIM PATTISON GROUP

Guinness World Records Limited has a very thorough accreditation system for records verification. However, while every effort is made to ensure accuracy, Guinness World Records Limited cannot be held responsible for any errors contained in this work. Feedback from our readers on any point of accuracy is always welcomed.

Guinness World Records Limited uses both metric and imperial measurements. The sole exceptions are for some scientific data where metric measurements only are universally accepted, and for some sports data. Where a specific date is given, the exchange rate is calculated according to the currency values that were in operation at the time. Where only a year date is given, the exchange rate is calculated from 31 Dec of that year. "1 billion" is taken to mean one thousand million.

Appropriate advice should always be taken when attempting to break or set records. Participants undertake records entirely at their own risk. Guinness World Records Limited has complete discretion over whether or not to include any particular record attempts in any of its publications. Being a Guinness World Records record holder does not guarantee you a place in any Guinness World Records publication.